Fashions of a Decade
The 1930s

Fashions of a Decade
The 1930s

Maria Costantino

CHELSEA HOUSE
PUBLISHERS
An imprint of Infobase Publishing

Chelsea House
An imprint of Infobase Publishing
132 West 31st Street
New York NY 10001

Library of Congress Cataloging-in-Publication Data
Costantino, Maria.
Fashions of a decade. The 1930s/Maria Costantino.
   p. cm.
   Includes bibliographical references and index
   ISBN 0-8160-6719-8 (alk. paper)
1. Clothing and dress—History—20th century—Juvenile literature. 2. Fashion—History—20th century—Juvenile literature. I. Title.
GT596.C67   2006
391.009/043—dc22   2006049933

Chelsea House books are available at special discounts when purchased in bulk quantities for businesses, associations, institutions, or sales promotions. Please call our Special Sales Department in New York at (212) 967-8800 or (800) 322-8755.

You can find Chelsea House on the World Wide Web at
http://www.chelseahouse.com

Author: Maria Costantino
Research for new edition: Kathy Elgin
Editor: Karen Taschek
Text design by Simon Borrough
Cover design by Dorothy M. Preston
Illustrations by Robert Price
Picture Research by Shelley Noronha

This new edition produced for Chelsea House by
Bailey Publishing Associates Ltd.

Printed in China through Morris Press, Ltd.

CP SB 10 9 8 7 6 5 4 3 2 1

This book is printed on acid-free paper.

Contents

THE 30s

The thirties were a decade that opened in depression and ended in war. Throughout the 1920s, economies worldwide had been booming, bringing prosperity to thousands of ordinary people who gambled their spare cash on stocks and shares. But in 1929, the economy of the Western world sank deep into a period of depression.

The downward spiral began with an excess of agricultural products, which led to falling prices. In an attempt to control the decline, produce was kept off the markets. The fall in agricultural prices meant that the farming population faced a reduced income. When agricultural prices began to fall, in America at least, investors in industry remained optimistic, and in early 1929, the price of stocks was still rising. With this investment in industry, manufacturers were able to increase their output: in 1929, the automobile industry produced about 5.5 million cars. But the industrialists soon began to realize that the market would become saturated and they would have to check production. Doubts turned into fears, which in turn grew into panic as people raced to withdraw their investments. On October 24, 1929, 13 million shares were sold on Wall Street, the financial heart of America. One company after another crashed as its credit failed, and by the end of the month, American investors had lost some $40 billion.

Unemployment rose while purchasing power collapsed. Large businesses failed, often taking smaller ones with them. Thousands of small investors lost everything, and in the industrialized towns and cities, unemployed workers joined breadlines. By 1932, 3 million were out of work in Britain, 6 million in Germany, and 14 million in the United States.

Generally, when we think of the 1930s, our minds conjure up images of despair: mass unemployment and breadlines, the rise of Fascism and the drift toward World War II. With these images firmly planted in our minds, it is easy to forget that fashion, beauty, and glamour were still important aspects of everyday life for many people.

Mickey Mouse and Snow White

Walt Disney's rise to fame is a classic success story. Born in 1901, a poor boy from the Midwest, he made his way to the top through a combination of enterprise, ingenuity, and hard work.

In 1928, Disney's finest creation, Mickey Mouse, made his debut in *Steamboat Willie*, the first cartoon to feature a fully synchronized sound track.

By the end of 1930, Mickey was an international celebrity, known in Italy as "Topolino" and in Japan as "Miki Kuchi." He was such a personality that in 1931, *Time* magazine ran a feature article on him. Equally remarkable was that Walt Disney had reached a position of eminence matching that of the greatest Hollywood stars and directors with only a handful of films, none of which ran for longer than eight minutes.

Influential admirers included the Italian conductor Arturo Toscanini and Russian film director Sergei Eisenstein.

Disney's first full-length animated film, *Snow White and the Seven Dwarfs*, which had cost close to $1.5 million, premiered on Christmas 1937 before a star-studded audience at Hollywood's Cathay Circle Theater. Sensational reviews followed, and *Snow White* went on to become not only a hit but a movie classic.

◀ **Mickey Mouse merchandise was everywhere in the thirties.**

Tightening the Belt

If fashion had been merely a luxury, during the 1930s the industry would have totally collapsed. Instead, it responded to all the economic and social changes of the decade and was swayed by the opposing influences of the economic climate and the impact of Hollywood-style luxury.

Because the rich were tightening their belts, spending less and making economies where they could, designers responded by cutting their prices, by producing new lines of ready-to-wear clothes to make up for the shortfall in orders for couture garments, and by producing more practical clothes made of economical and washable fabrics. In 1931, Gabrielle "Coco" Chanel showed a collection of evening dresses that helped to promote cotton as a fashion fabric, and by 1932, she had also cut nearly 50 percent off her prices.

Designers also had new fabrics to work with. What were then called artificial silks like rayon were now stronger and better, and in 1939, the production of nylon began in the United States. Nylon was stronger and more elastic than previous artificial silks. In addition to a whole host of preshrunk, or Sanforized, fabrics, there were uncrushable fabrics like Zingale and glass fabrics like Rhodophane, which Elsa Schiaparelli used to sensational effect.

For women who could afford them, the fashions of the early thirties were stylish and elegant. The longer and more flowing lines that the Paris-based couturiers had shown in their collections in the autumn of 1929 were to become established in 1930. But the increasingly difficult economic situation meant that many women simply could not afford the luxury of new clothes. In an effort to bring their existing shorter-length skirts up

▼These 1932 dinner frocks from the House of Lelong show fashion in a transitional phase. The longer length and slimmer cut are countered by the crisscross necklines, which still retain a feel of the previous decade.

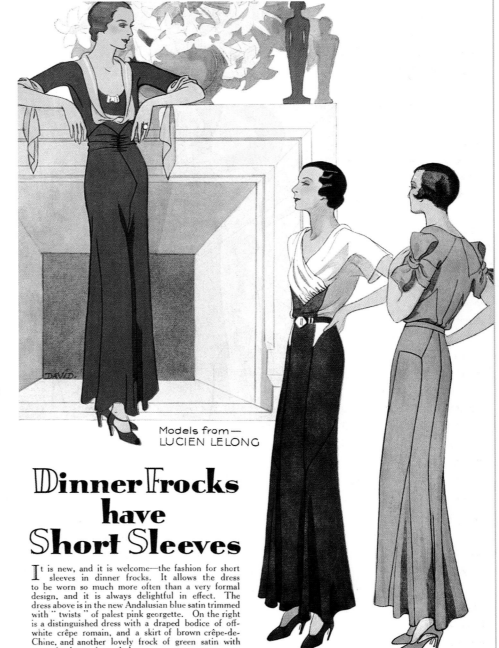

Models from—
LUCIEN LELONG

Dinner Frocks have Short Sleeves

It is new, and it is welcome—the fashion for short sleeves in dinner frocks. It allows the dress to be worn so much more often than a very formal design, and it is always delightful in effect. The dress above is in the new Andalusian blue satin trimmed with " twists " of palest pink georgette. On the right is a distinguished dress with a draped bodice of off-white crêpe romain, and a skirt of brown crêpe-de-Chine, and another lovely frock of green satin with attractive bow-trimmed sleeves.

New Deal

On a cold, windy day, March 4, 1933, Franklin Delano Roosevelt took the presidential oath of office and addressed America with the words: "This great nation will endure as it has endured, will revive and will prosper." Roosevelt seemed to promise, as his popular campaign song indicated, "Happy Days Are Here Again."

The plan to revive the flagging American economy and national spirit was called the New Deal, and the president's first act was to rescue the banks, many of which had gone into bankruptcy. In the first of his famous Fireside Chats on the radio, FDR announced that the banks would reopen the next day. All over America, people listening in were convinced of his ability to lead them out of the Depression: the next day, bank deposits exceeded withdrawals.

A more lighthearted way of cheering up the country was the repeal of the Eighteenth Amendment, which since 1920 had prohibited the manufacture and sale of alcohol.

But FDR did not lose sight of the many other important issues. The New Deal program of reforms brought help for mortgaged farmers and tenants by ensuring that their mortgage holders and landlords did not foreclose and leave them homeless. A federal payroll of $500 million was used to put the unemployed back to work. On Muscle Shoals in Tennessee, the river was used to generate cheap electrical power for the people of the Tennessee Valley.

The New Deal program had something for everyone: farmers, workers—even writers and artists, with a government-sponsored program of public art and writing projects. All this reflected Roosevelt's hope that he could lead a united country along the road to recovery.

▲From 1934 through the late 1930s, the Midwest was hit by annual dust storms, with huge black clouds of soil blowing off farmland that had been overplanted and overgrazed. Destitute farmers headed west to California, which they believed to be a promised land with jobs for all.

▲Marathon dancing was a grim way for the desperate to earn money in the Depression. Couples danced for days on end until the last left standing won a cash prize. The authorities tried to close these dances down, but audiences loved them.

to date, many women resorted to adding lengthening bands of contrasting fabric or even fur to their hems. Material was often added to collars and sleeves to give the impression that their outfit had been designed that way and was not simply an emergency measure.

Within a year, the new lines for fashion had been established, and as if they were mirroring the economic slump, hemlines dropped. Longer and narrower skirts that gradually flared out fell to the bottom of the calf. Longer hair was waved lower onto the nape of the neck. Hats featured skullcaps with draped folds of fabric attached to the back or sides or brims that obscured one eye. Sleeves were now full from the elbow to the wrist, where they draped onto cuffs or were loosely tied.

Colors also reflected the subdued mood of the early thirties: black, navy, and gray were popular for city wear; browns and greens were popular for autumn outfits. For afternoon wear and evening dresses, black or pastel shades of peach, pink, green, and blue were the most fashionable.

The Material Sets the Hour

Models — LELONG

For the morning a dress of Bordeaux red Madiana. The fall of the collar on this neat dress, the bow, and the looped basque effect are all new and interesting. The shoulders are cut to look broad, and the waist is well defined. For the afternoon there is the coat and dress of crêpe marocain in beige and nigger brown. In this you see how cleverly contrast can be used to give an outline which is slender. The dark bands down the arms and on the front of the coat give a deceptive outline. For the evening, Lelong makes this frock of sea blue lace. It is the kind of dress that looks as charming at an informal dinner as in a ballroom, since its uncommon puff sleeves are smart enough for any gathering, yet are also the reason for labelling the dress " informal."

No paper patterns can be obtained of these Paris models

45

Moving with the Movies

Although designers still continued to create lavish gowns for royalty and the rich, they were also taking into account the requirements of the working lives led by more and more ordinary women. The changed role of women in society and the gradual weakening of clearly defined social distinctions that had begun at the beginning of the century meant that many more people were sharing similar lifestyles. During the day, women might be working in offices or in light industry, while their evenings were spent dancing or at the theater or movies.

If radio was the miracle of the twenties, the miracle of the thirties was the talking picture. Sound movies had arrived in 1927, but it was in the thirties that they were truly "all talking, all singing, all dancing" spectaculars. While the rich and royal may still have looked to Paris for their fashions, working women all over the world—and even the couturiers themselves—kept an eye on the movies.

▲More outfits from Lucien Lelong, for (right to left) morning, afternoon, and evening. The overall shape of all three designs is defined by broad shoulders and narrow waists, as well as contrasting effects of texture and color.

▲The text on this ad read: "Whether she speaks English, French, Spanish, Italian, or Yankee Americanese . . . her gown proclaims in the very shade and texture of its fabric the worldwide preference for Stehli Silk." The favorite fabric of a decade that loved bias cuts and folds, nothing would cut and drape like silk.

◀ The relative simplicity of Greta Garbo's style ensured that she achieved popularity while maintaining her air of mystery and aloofness. Photo in *Red Letter* magazine, 1933.

▶ "Watching a Joan Crawford film is like flipping through a 1934 issue of *Vogue*," wrote one critic about the woman who played tough but was never less than elegant.

▲ Claudette Colbert had a special talent for comedy in addition to dramatic roles. Despite her fluffy image, she had good business sense and was one of Hollywood's highest-paid stars of the late 1930s.

The first of the designers to try to join movie costumes with real-life clothes was Coco Chanel, who went to Hollywood in 1929. Although her designs were elegant and innovative, by the time the movies were released, hemlines had dropped and the styles that she had created were obsolete. Nevertheless, many other designers made the pilgrimage across the Atlantic to Hollywood, including Elsa Schiaparelli, Marcel Rochas, Captain Edward Molyneux, Alix (later Madame Grès), Jean Patou, and Jeanne Lanvin. But undoubtedly the best were Hollywood's own indigenous designers like Gilbert Adrian, Orry-Kelly, and Edith Head.

Not only did women copy the dress styles of the movie stars, they also copied their hair. Claudette Colbert's bangs, created by Hollywood stylist Antoine, became popular. Greta Garbo's bobbed hairstyle was another Antoine creation. Women all over the world now started to copy the style by parting their

Ya Ain't Heard Nothin' Yet

After the 1927 success of the first "all singing, all talking" movie *The Jazz Singer*, which starred Al Jolson as the son of a Jewish cantor who embarks on a career as a music hall singer, Hollywood soon realized that movie audiences would no longer pay to see silent movies.

Many of the silent screen stars were unable to make the transition from silent movie acting to the more subtle style required by sound pictures. They were now required to act and deliver their lines without interruption from the director, who had previously been able to shout out instructions on the set. Good voices and clear pronunciation were now a must, which meant that stage-trained actors rapidly replaced silent stars. Many actors ended their careers either because they had strong foreign accents (like Pola Negri and Emil Jannings) or voices that somehow did not match their screen image (like Norma Talmadge and screen idol John Gilbert).

Other silent stars, like Greta Garbo, Gary Cooper, Janet Gaynor, and Joan Crawford made the transition to sound movies with the help of voice teachers and dialogue coaches.

Advances in sound also led to the rise of an important new genre, the musical. At first, musicals were simply filmed versions of Broadway shows, but within a few years, thanks largely to the work of two men—choreographer Busby Berkeley (1895–1976) and dancer-choreographer Fred Astaire (1899–1987)—the original movie musical grew in sophistication to become the film hit of the 1930s.

hair either in the center or on the side and waving or curling their hair onto their shoulders. Another variation was the long bob, created by pinning up the front and sides of the hair and leaving the back loose or curled under on the shoulder like a long pageboy style.

Thanks to Hollywood, the cosmetic industry began to evolve into the giant it is today. Innovations in these years included false fingernails and eyelashes. Unlike the twenties, when makeup features in magazines had been rare, every important movie star now appeared in fan and fashion magazines and contributed to the new looks with step-by-step guides to transforming one's self from girl next door to glamour girl—with the help of face makeup, eye shadows, pencils, mascara, rouge, and the very essential lipstick. In their efforts to look more like the Hollywood stars, women copied Marlene Dietrich's practice of plucking her eyebrows to the thinnest line. If their own eyebrows were not arched enough, they plucked them off completely and penciled in new super-thin arched brows.

Fashion photographers like Cecil Beaton, Horst P. Horst, Man Ray, and George Hoyningen-Heune also caught the Hollywood fever and photographed their models in a movie-like style, re-creating the rich tones, highlights, and mood of movies.

The Modern Woman

The new woman of the thirties was also a different shape. Gone was the flat-chested, boyish look of the previous decade. Bosoms reappeared, waists were back in their normal place, and shoulders gradually began to broaden—eventually reaching the exaggerated proportions of Joan Crawford's. Curves returned as skirts were draped over hips. But the biggest fashion innovation of the decade was the backless evening gown. Popularly accredited to French couturier Madame Madeleine Vionnet, the halter-neck, bias-cut evening gowns shaped themselves to the wearer's body.

With a variety of outfits, women naturally needed a variety of shoes. In the twenties, shoe designs had been limited for the most part to "Louis-heeled" styles (resembling those worn by the French king) with pointed toes for evening wear and sturdier versions for day wear. Thirties shoes came in a variety of styles, heel heights, and materials, with pumps popular for both day (in crocodile, lizard, and snakeskin) and evening (in satins, dyed to match evening gowns, brocades, and silver or gold kid).

Sandals were also popular and were worn with sundresses and beach pajamas. Beach pajamas were oufits of flapping, bell-bottomed pants plus a loose top that could be worn over a swimsuit to cover modest ladies as they journeyed from their hotel to the beach or the cabin of their cruise liner to the sundeck. Pants had been worn by the more avant-garde fashion-conscious woman in the late 1920s, but by the thirties, they were more acceptable and more widely adopted.

Sandals came in a variety of styles: sling-back, high-heeled, open-toed—and in 1936, Italian shoe designer Salvatore Ferragamo introduced the wedge heel, followed in 1938 by the platform sole. It was even possible to produce combinations: open-toed, sling-back platform wedges!

By 1939, daytime shoes had developed into practical, low-heeled, broad-toed shoes of rather clumpy design. It would be some years before many women would have the opportunity to wear more dainty styles.

▲ *Footlight Parade*, from 1933, shows off the Busby Berkeley babes to perfection.

Hats Off to Busby!

A successful dance director cf Broadway shows, Busby Berkeley went to Hollywood in 1930 to work for Samuel Goldwyn, but it was not until 1933, when Berkeley moved to the Warner Brothers studio, that his true genius was revealed. As dance director for movie musicals like *42nd Street, Footlight Parade, Dames*, and the "Gold Digger" films of 1933, 1935, 1937, and 1938, Berkley developed his flamboyant visual style with the help of aerial photography, kaleidoscopic camera lenses, and scores of singers and dancers.

►"Style and Home," German style, from 1932. In particular, note the collar detail and asymmetrical fastening.

▼The sophistication of these Ferragamo platform shoes from the late thirties makes us forget that the designer got his big break by designing footwear for "sword and sandal" epics in the 1920s.

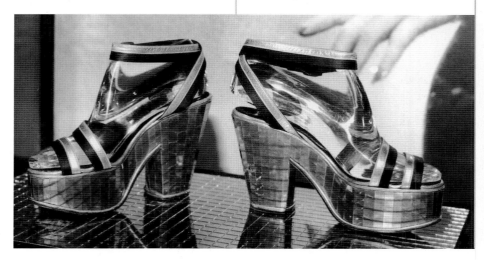

Mode und Heim

...sgabe mit Versicherung

▲Shoes for day wear were neat but unexciting. The hand-fashioned Spring range from Lotus featured a high-heeled suede court shoe, a shoe with punched-out designs, and two heeled lace-ups.

►Pleats from the knee, cloche hats, and contrasting weaves were the hallmark of late thirties day wear by Captain Edward Molyneux, a British designer working in Paris.

▼A huge number of movie magazines kept fans abreast of the fashions of their heroines.

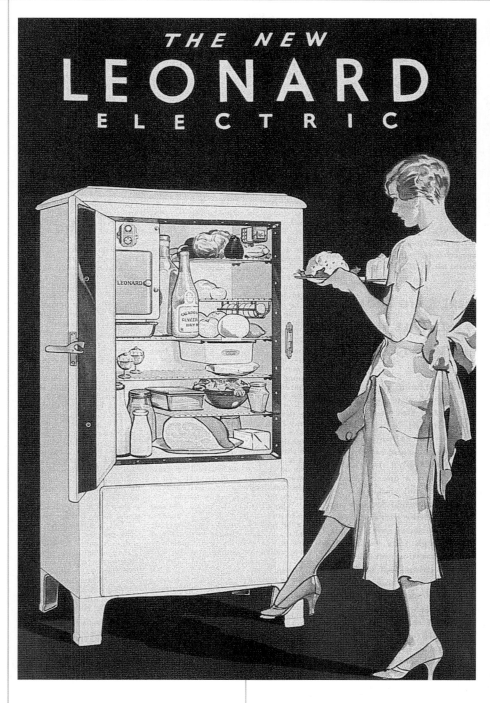

THE NEW
LEONARD
ELECTRIC

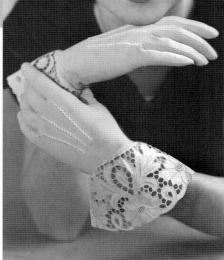

▲These French gauntlet-style gloves from 1934 have elegant cutwork at the wrist and would probably be worn for taking afternoon tea in town.

Vital Accessories

While the wealthier woman might own a number of outfits suitable for many different occasions, to a vast number of women the world of fashion clothing was unattainable. Many women simply had to make their clothes last longer, and wherever possible, they altered them by adding new trimmings to hats and coats and new collars and cuffs to dresses. Although the styles of the early thirties were more complicated to make and required more fabric than the simple short, straight-lined styles of the 1920s, resourceful home knitters and dressmakers still managed to look fashionable. Separates like knitwear, blouses,

▲Laborsaving devices, like the electric refrigerator, made their appearance in the home, allowing the housewife to prepare meals, and apparently, finish all her housework dressed as if for a party.

skirts, and button-up dresses became the foundation on which many women built a fashionable image. A change of hairstyle or a new scarf, bag, or brooch helped to keep up appearances and spirits.

The large department stores catered to the modern woman's needs. Not only would she find the basic household goods, furnishings, and clothing under one roof—here the fashionable woman could also buy those important little items that finished off her outfit.

DC·15

DC·16

DC·17

DC·18

DC·19

DC·20

DC·21

DC·22

DC·23

DC·24

▲ A selection of British and European handbags from 1933. *Pochettes* (small bags) and evening bags in crepe de chine sit alongside a beaded bag, an embroidered nightgown sachet, and a bag with appliqué flowers.

►These three girls with their perky little hats are described as "of the Ginger Rogers era," indicating just how much influence the dancing star had on the fashions of the day (*see page 31*).

▲Even today, the best straw hats come from Italy, where they have been made since the sixteenth century. Most people have probably forgotten by now that the word milliner is a corruption of "Milan," the town at the center of the hat industry.

Costume jewelry in semiprecious stones or even fake plastic had been popular since the twenties, and by the thirties, costume jewelry departments in stores could be extensive. Rhinestones and diamanté earrings and clip sets were popular. Most fashionable were heart-shaped or stud earrings, while the dress clips were often larger versions of the same shape. These clips were worn fastened to scarves or collars and sometimes worn as a pair on the neckline of a dress. Placed at either side of the neckline, the clips pulled the neck of a dress open and down, forming a diamond or heart shape—the so-called sweetheart neckline.

Belts, handbags, and hats were also very important parts of an outfit. Autumn and winter styles for hats were based on rather masculine shapes, with high crowns trimmed with a matching or contrasting band of ribbon. Tyrolean-style hats with feather trims or veils were also popular. Hats with curled or shovel-fronted brims were worn tilted on the forehead and turned up at the back to reveal neatly waved or roll-curled hairstyles. In the summer, shiny straw hats were the most popular. These were usually fairly large saucer shapes trimmed with artificial fruit or flowers and worn at an angle. Often an elastic band was attached to the inside of the crown and pulled over the back of the head to hold the hat in position, the band concealed under the waves of the hair.

Gloves were selected with great care to complement each outfit. With city clothes, suede or soft kid leather wrist gauntlets or elbow-length gloves would be worn. More expensive gloves had scalloped edges and embroidered details. Less fancy short gloves in leather, wool, or combinations of the two were worn with more casual country clothes, while knitted gloves with fancy patterns and colors were popular with home knitters, younger girls, and winter sports fans.

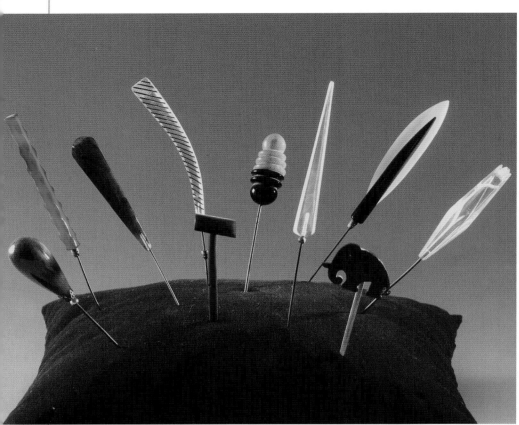

◄ A selection of Art Deco hat pins with stylized plastic heads.

►A recruiting poster for the Hitler Youth association.

Jugend dient dem Führer

Hitler and the Nazis

Adolf Hitler was no ordinary political leader. Nor did the Nazi Party conduct itself like a traditional political party. The Nazis placed great emphasis on visual and verbal impact, using uniforms, the swastika emblem, mass rallies, and constantly repeated slogans. Political meetings were huge, cleverly stage-managed public events. But the Nazis kept their message simple: Germany was the rightful ruler of Central and Eastern Europe; traitors both inside and outside Germany had caused its defeat in 1918 and had since conspired to keep Germany weak. The Nazis demanded that these traitors be replaced with "loyal" Germans like themselves so that Germany could once again be strong.

Hitler was convinced that leadership was being denied him by an international conspiracy of Jews and Communists. He also believed that when different races intermarry, they become degenerate, so in order to safeguard the "purity" of the Germans, he adopted a policy of anti-Semitism. Persecution of Jews began soon after the Nazis came to power.

Each time a woman changed her clothes, she changed her handbag. Small, neat bags continued to be popular with evening dresses, but as the daytime silhouette became fuller, larger bags became more fashionable. Large, thin envelope bags were held under one arm; in contrast, very soft leather or suede was draped onto an often elaborately worked clasp to give a classical draped style to a bag, which hung from the arm on broad straps. For summer wear, handbags were made in linen or straw with appliquéd or embroidered motifs to match dress colors and fabrics.

Body-conscious and health-conscious men and women took to physical fitness in droves, dressed in knee-length shorts and sports shirts made of open-weave fabrics. The ultimate fashion accessory of the thirties was a suntan—preferably, for Europeans, gained at one of the fashionable French resorts of Le Touquet, Cannes, or Biarritz.

Throughout history, fashion had dictated that suntans were undesirable since they were associated with outdoor work and hence peasant life. Fashionable women had always tried to keep their complexions as pale as possible by covering up their skin under skirts, hats, and sunshades. In the late twenties, Coco Chanel started the vogue for sunbathing, and it was during this time that a suntan became synonymous not with work but with leisure. Naturally, sunbathing produced the need for yet another fashion accessory—sunglasses, which were quickly popularized by the Hollywood stars.

►America's Jesse Owens leads the field on his way to winning the gold medal in the 200 meters at the Berlin Olympic Games, 1936.

Berlin Olympics

In 1936, it was the turn of Germany and the city of Berlin to host the Olympic Games. Hitler attempted to turn the entire occasion into a spectacular display of Germanic, or Aryan, superiority and the will to win of the "master race."

Unfortunately for Hitler, black American athlete Jesse Owens made a mockery of his racial policies by winning four gold medals and breaking two world records. Hitler refused to present Owens with his medals.

Hitler had commissioned the German filmmaker Leni Riefenstahl to make a spectacular documentary of the 1936 game, and despite the poor showing of the Aryan athletes, *Olympiad/Olympic* was finally released in 1938. Although it is a testament to athletic achievement, it was also a strong propaganda piece for Hitler's Germany, maintaining that good health and physical well-being were by-products of Nazism.

►This poster advertises the Winter Olympics, held in Munich in 1936 to complement the summer games in Berlin. The skier is sporting the latest—and, for the period—formfitting ski wear.

DEUTSCHLAND 1936
IV·OLYMPISCHE WINTERSPIELE
GARMISCH-PARTENKIRCHEN
6·16 FEBRUAR 1936

◀ In that famous phrase, Edward G. Robinson tells partygoers to "reach for the sky" in a scene from *Little Caesar* (1930).

Little Caesars

The coming of sound in the movies and the new "realism" it allowed also gave rise to a cycle of gangster movies that vividly portrayed armed violence and tough talk. Between 1930 and 1933, the brutal violence of films like *Little Caesar*, *Public Enemy*, and *Scarface* provoked a public outcry.

In 1933, the Hays Office, under the supervision of Postmaster General Will Hays, intervened with the Production Code Administration, intended to impose certain standards on motion picture producers.

In addition to prohibiting "scenes of passion," unpunished acts of adultery or seduction, profane and vulgar language—like the words "guts" and "nuts"—nudity, cruelty to animals and children, or any representations of childbirth, the Hays Code outlawed depictions of certain types of crime. Gangster films could no longer show machine guns or even allow screen gangsters to mention weapons. Law enforcement agents must never be shown dying at the hands of criminals, and all criminal activities must be seen to be duly punished.

The response to these restrictions was a shift in emphasis from the gangster as tragic hero to the gangster as social victim. This led to a spate of films like William Wyler's *Dead End* (1937), Fritz Lang's *You Only Live Once* (1937), and Michael Curtiz's *Angels with Dirty Faces* (1938), set in deprived neighborhoods and often involving prison.

Rising Sun

America and Europe alike were uncertain about what steps should be taken to halt the political trends in Europe in the thirties. Both were, however, becoming increasingly anti-Nazi, a process that was encouraged by Germany's association with Japan. Germany and Japan were seen as power hungry, promoting oppressive domestic policies and external aggression. In 1936, Japan and Germany signed the Anti-Comintern Pact, agreeing to exchange information about international Communist activities and cooperate in planning counter-measures.

In 1931, Japan's increasing need for economic recovery after the Depression, its need for raw materials for industry, and the ambitions of its political and military leaders converged. Japan invaded Manchuria, in China, on the pretext of protecting the economic interests of the Japanese-owned South Manchurian Railway Company.

While Japanese diplomats assured foreign statesmen that the military operations were a temporary measure and that their troops would be withdrawn as soon as possible, the advance of the Japanese forces in China continued unabated. It became clear that Japan was a threat to the Asian colonies and spheres of influence established by the European powers in earlier centuries. Japan would see war in Europe as a green light to seize these colonies.

▼In this cover illustration by Ernst Dryden for the February 1932 issue of the fashionable French men's magazine *Adam*, a man in studiedly casual clothes lounges around a harbor or boating marina.

ADAM
LA REVUE DE L'HOMME.

8e ANNÉE — N° 70.
15 FÉVRIER 1932
PRIX : 6 FRS

Fashion for Everyone

Being fashionable was not, of course, simply confined to the ladies. Men's clothes were also heavily influenced by royalty and movie stars.

With the exception of colored sports clothing, men's clothes in the thirties were quite dull. Setting the trend for menswear in this decade was the Prince of Wales, later King Edward VIII—the man who would give up the throne of England to marry ultra-fashionable American divorcée Mrs. Wallis Simpson. The Prince of Wales set the trend for American-style trousers, wide-legged pants fitting snugly around the hips. For evening, he revived the fashion for wearing white vests under his dinner jacket.

For men, a broader figure with wide shoulders and an athletic look was much admired. Sensing the changing mood, Hollywood studios made fewer films featuring the romantic, sensitive heroes popular with female audiences in the 1920s. Men were now portrayed in more masculine and earthy ways. Movies with war themes became popular, with the male lead playing the role of a dashing, daring pilot. The men who portrayed gangsters in the movies may not have been as good-looking as earlier stars, but they were now the tough guys: he-men and strong, silent types. In an effort to impress their sweethearts, many young men took to wearing long, loose overcoats or raincoats with the collars turned up—a style heavily influenced by screen gangsters like George Raft or the emerging Humphrey Bogart.

Men's clothes were very conservative compared to women's. Business and social etiquette still required men to wear heavy, dark suits, collars, and ties—and, of course, a hat. The most popular hat of the thirties was the trilby, a soft felt hat with an indented crown, made fashionable by Sir Antony Eden, the British statesman.

◄ George Raft, another of the screen "gangsters" who really dressed to kill. Note the elegant leather gloves in this shot from *They Drive by Night*, made at the end of the decade.

An alternative was the fedora, a hat with "snap" brim that was worn with the brim up at the back and down at the front.

Many of the younger generation, especially the more bohemian artists and writers, were very politically conscious, and their clothing often displayed their beliefs. Since they felt that dealing with serious world problems was more important than spending time and money on their appearance, the clothes they wore were basic and functional.

Young women in this group wore their hair straight and cut off at the chin or shoulder: longer hair was pinned up into a bun or worn in braids. Young men still wore their hair short, but it was considered longer and less well groomed than was usual or acceptable for the thirties. Many of these men discarded their hats, but some did wear berets, as did like-minded females. Young women sometimes wore scarves tied either under the chin or at the back of the neck in what was considered a peasant style. For both the men and women of the "hatless brigade," standard clothing consisted of basic and often leather jackets, open-necked shirts or roll-neck sweaters, and baggy corduroy trousers. Well-polished lace-up shoes were cast aside in favor of sensible and comfortable open-toed sandals.

Children were not immune from fashion, especially the well-known ones. The two young British princesses Elizabeth and Margaret Rose were followed, photographed, and copied everywhere they went. In 1932, little girls in England all wanted a "Margaret Rose dress": a knitted dress trimmed with rosebuds. Following a newspaper report that Princess Elizabeth's favorite colors were primrose yellow and pink, lots of little girls went to parties swathed in tiered organdy dresses in the colors worn by the future queen of England.

The child idols of Hollywood were Judy Garland, Mickey Rooney, and Shirley Temple, whose curls and sweetness won the hearts of millions of mothers. There was even a product called Curly Top, which claimed to encourage children's hair to curl! Boys, however, had their curls cut off and were dressed in miniature men's suits and ties as soon as they were old enough.

▼Style for girls. Shirley Temple stars in *Curly Top,* complete with fashionable box-pleat skirt and fitted capelet with hand-embroidered ducks. The outfit was designed by Rene Hubert, wardrobe chief for Twentieth Century Fox.

The Spanish Civil War

In 1936, the army, under the leadership of the Fascist General Francisco Franco, led a revolt against Spain's legitimately elected left-wing government, attempting to replace it with a single-party, conservative, and Catholic state.

The government had the support of republicans, socialists, communists, anarchists, labor groups, and Catalan and Basque nationalists, all organized into a loose coalition calling themselves Loyalists. They were soon joined by a volunteer force of men and women from other countries—including many writers and artists—known as the International Brigade. The contingent of 3,000 American volunteers was known as the Abraham Lincoln Brigade.

Both Italy and Germany supported Franco, providing thousands of their own troops, advisers, planes, tanks, and ammunition. Only Russia gave any help to the Loyalists, while democratic governments in America and Europe chose neutrality. In spring 1939, however, the Russians stopped supplying the Loyalists, and the Spanish Republic finally fell after more than two years of bloodshed. More than a million Spaniards had died, and thousands of refugees had fled to France.

One of the worst incidents was in 1937, when the German Luftwaffe bombed the small Basque town of Guernica in northern Spain, inflicting massive civilian casualties. Such horrifying scenes of death and destruction finally made all nations aware that warfare was no longer limited solely to opposing armies. Civilians—even whole civilizations—were now under threat from the machinery of modern warfare.

From Munich to World War II

Hitler's plans for a greater Germany implied expansion into neighboring territories, and by 1938, he was threatening Czechoslovakia (now the Czech Republic and Slovakia). In an attempt to appease Hitler and prevent him invading the whole country, the Sudetenland—the area of Czechoslovakia that bordered Germany and contained many German-speaking Czechs—was ceded to Germany in the Munich Agreement of September 1938. Signing the treaty, British prime minister Neville Chamberlain promised that it guaranteed "peace in our time."

Peace, however, proved to be a short-lived respite during which the major European countries continued their massive rearmament. In March 1939, Germany annexed the remainder of Czechoslovakia, and in August, negotiations between Britain, France, and the Soviet Union to form a "peace bloc" broke down when the USSR signed a non-aggression pact with Germany.

On September 1, Hitler's armies invaded Poland, and two days later, Britain and France declared war on Germany. The conflict would last until 1945 and claim some 20 million lives around the globe.

▼Pablo Picasso's *Guernica* has become the single most telling symbol of the Spanish Civil War.

Wallis and the King

Mrs. Wallis Simpson, the wealthy American divorcee whose marriage to the Prince of Wales, heir to the British throne, caused a major constitutional crisis, was famous as a fashionable trendsetter. Her extensive jewelry collection was auctioned after her death for a record-breaking sum.

Spirit of the Age

Hollywood and royalty were not the only influences on fashion design in the thirties. Designers also responded to the current trends in art, science, and even engineering. One major art and literary movement of the thirties was Surrealism, which featured dream-like landscapes and strange images. The motifs used by Surrealist artists like Salvador Dalí, René Magritte, Max Ernst, Jean Cocteau, and Man Ray can be found incorporated into many designs by couturiers—especially those of Elsa Schiaparelli, who often collaborated with Surrealist artists to produce hats that looked like shoes or wicker baskets filled with butterflies, dresses with "desk drawers," and gloves with gold fingernails attached to them.

The 1930s were also a decade of great engineering triumphs, symbolized best in the early years by the Chrysler Building and the Empire State Building in New York City and later, in 1937, by San Francisco's Golden Gate Bridge. While some people attempted to produce the tallest, the largest, or the biggest, others competed for the honor of being the fastest. The idea of speed captured the imagination of young people in the thirties and led to fierce international competition for all types of speed records, like the fastest transatlantic crossing by an ocean liner. World land speed records were set and broken by Britain's Sir Malcolm Campbell in his car Bluebird, while in the air, his compatriot Amy Johnson flew her tiny Gypsy Moth plane called Jason from Europe to Australia. When *Vogue* announced in 1934 that the fashionable silhouette would have the sleek lines of a speedboat or airplane, evening dresses fell into swallowtail points at the back, waists were pinched in, hair was swept back, and hats were cut across the head at acute angles.

But in 1939, it was to be all change on the fashion front. As Europe became embroiled in World War II, fashion designers and magazines stressed economy, simplicity, and practicality. For many women, the clothes they had bought in 1939 were the last they would invest in for a long time. Now they had to make do and mend.

◄ In their wedding picture, Mrs. Simpson shows her flair for fashion in a dress from American designer Mainbocher. Telltale details include the gathered bodice and tiny ornamental buttons.

▲ Almost dwarfed by a streamlined locomotive, a model in fox fur jacket and "bird hat" by Elsa Schiaparelli makes the cover of *Vogue*, fall 1939. Look closely to see the model's oversized bangle bracelets.

Dancing in the Depression

Gowns to Beat the Blues

Despite failing economies, many women saw it as their duty to be fashionable. As people tried to compensate for the grayness of everyday life in the Depression, they turned their leisure time into something special by way of their clothes.

Evening clothes became very different from day clothes. In earlier decades, when the wealthy had set the styles, there had been no real need for them to wear practical day clothes or to reserve the really impractical styles for evening. Now, despite the Depression, all kinds of women were leading active and productive lives. They required simpler fashions for daily wear, while their luxurious long gowns were kept for evening. Evening dress for men remained formal: dinner jacket, tuxedo, or tails.

Summer in Tov...

Left: Two afternoon outfits, the first in a pa... beige crêpe de chine with darker beige spo... the coat trimmed with blue fox. The second black crêpe with white spots and green wi... white spots; white hat and collar

Three versions of the useful straw boater hat, showing the variations in the sizes of the crown

▲ A more elegant chain store look for 1939, with tightly belted waists and gathered sleeves. Hats could be wide brimmed or narrow, as long as they were worn at a saucy angle.

◄ American tailoring is seen at its best in these custom-made suits from Middishade. The catalog for 1931 offered Middishade Blue, Gray, and Brown.

▲Tailor-made clothes for spring 1932 from Lucile of Paris. The dress on the left, trimmed with four brass buttons, is worn over a beige "chemisette." A boldly colored scarf contrasts with the blue-and-white diagonals of the center dress, while the jacket of the beige suit on the right falls to a point at the back, and its collar and cuffs are trimmed with brown astrakhan.

▲The styles for fall 1933 are defined by subdued colors, asymmetrical fastenings, three-quarter-length skirts, fur trimmings, tiny clutch bags, and berets.

In 1930, *Vogue* summed up the day and evening looks of the year. They all came from the Anglo-Danish actress Gertrude Lawrence's wardrobe for Noel Coward's play *Private Lives* and were designed by Paris-based American Mainbocher: fur-trimmed tweeds and a bias-cut evening dress of paneled white satin.

Peelin' the Apple

Suitably attired for the evening, people could escape the bleakness of everyday life at the theater, where they were captivated by the lyrics and melodies of Jerome Kern, Cole Porter, George Gershwin, and Noel Coward. But an even more popular entertainment in these years was dancing.

In the twenties, the popular dances had been the Charleston and the Black Bottom—but in the thirties, you needed rhythm and had to know how to "swing." The swing music of Americans like Fats Waller, Jack "The Gate" Teagarden ("gate" meaning the ability to swing), Count Basie, Artie Shaw, and Duke Ellington set dance floors humming, from the ritziest nightclubs and ocean liners right down to dance halls. Even in front of the radio in their own living rooms, everyone and anyone Lindy-Hopped or danced the Big Apple (the forerunner of the jitterbug, whose name

▼"Big band" was the definitive sound of the thirties.

was a euphemism meaning "bottom"). Dancing was a popular way to keep fit in the thirties. You needed more than rhythm for steps like Kicking the Mule, Truckin', and Peelin' the Apple: these dances also required complete unselfconsciousness. In America, this was no doubt encouraged by the repeal, in 1933, of Prohibition—a ban on the manufacture and sale of alcohol in place since 1920. The more restrained could still tango or take to the dance floor to the sounds of the big bands led by Henry Hall, Jack Payne, Glenn Miller, and Tommy and Jimmy Dorsey.

Offshoots of commercial swing music included Latin American rhythms like the rhumba, whose hip-swaying movements were ideal for drawing attention to the flowing lines of draped, bias-cut dresses. The more acrobatic Lindy Hoppers needed different dancing clothes—for women, blouses and sweaters with a short flared or pleated skirt, white bobby socks (ankle socks), and flat shoes. For their partners, the look was created by loose pants and sweaters.

The best loved of all the dancers were also Hollywood idols. Throughout the decade, Fred Astaire and Ginger Rogers dazzled audiences with their intricate routines and left everyone humming "Cheek to Cheek," the hit song from *Top Hat*. RKO had been one of the smallest of the Hollywood film studios, but in 1933, following the success of the first Fred Astaire and Ginger Rogers film, *Flying Down to Rio*—in which they weren't even given star billing—it became known as the home of the Fred Astaire-Ginger Rogers musical. Between 1934 and 1939, RKO made eight Astaire-Rogers movies, including *The Gay Divorcée* (1934), *Top Hat* (1935), and *Swing Time* (1936), establishing Fred and Ginger among the most popular box office attractions in America.

Although they both began as performers, Astaire went on to direct and choreograph most of his own dance sequences, while Ginger Rogers designed many of the lavish gowns she wore on-screen.

Gentlemen Drivers

Another popular way of keeping the blues at bay in the thirties was automobile driving. Those fortunate enough to own a car, whether it was a Ford "Tin Lizzie" or one of the fancier sports models, drove off to the new "roadhouses," some of which had restaurants and sometimes swimming pools and dance floors. For these outings, the chic woman wore a jacket-and-skirt outfit under one of the new three-quarter-length swagger coats with epaulets at the shoulders or, on wet days, a military-style trench coat.

Gentlemen drivers ideally sported heavily greased hair, a little mustache in the manner of Hollywood star Ronald Colman, a single-breasted jacket, and a pair of plus fours—a form of knickers—worn over diamond-patterned woolen stockings. The "lounge lizard" type—smooth and languid with clipped sideburns—wore cuff links, shirt studs, and tie pins and carried a cigarette holder.

Being correctly dressed for the occasion was not something dictated by fashion alone. In the thirties, social duty and status also demanded that the correct hats, dresses, or suits be worn. Suspenders and certain styles of boots and caps, were not acceptable. There might be a Depression but fashionable men and women could not drop their standards.

▲Few could match the style of Fred and Ginger, but the Lindy Hop was for everybody—or at least, the young and fit.

◄ Style was crucial, even in the suburbs: the DeSoto was billed as "America's smartest low-price car."

Hooray for Hollywood!

Stars of the Silver Screen

In the midst of pre-war gloom and the economic depression blazed the irresistible glamour of American films. The screen goddesses of the thirties—Joan Crawford, Greta Garbo, Jean Harlow, Marlene Dietrich, or Mae West—were models whose looks and mannerisms many women tried to copy. Furthermore, the cinema also acted as a showcase for chic, avant-garde interiors: there was a preference for films in which the settings were department stores, beauty salons, and glamorous homes. Shot in black and white, the Hollywood movies popularized the characteristic Art Deco style of the period.

Certain stars were style models, and the outfits they wore became important features of the film, exerting a direct influence on the fashions available in the stores. One of the top Hollywood designers was Gilbert Adrian, who had begun his West Coast career creating clothes for silent movie star Rudolph Valentino. Later, when Adrian joined MGM Studios, he designed costumes for Crawford, Harlow, and Norma Shearer. For Garbo, in the 1929 film *A Woman of Affairs*, he had created the "slouch hat," a larger-than-normal cloche hat worn at an angle and pulled down over the forehead. It proved to be influential on hat design for the next ten years. In 1936, Garbo wore another Adrian creation, the Eugenie hat in the film *Camille*. Trimmed with ostrich feathers and partially obscuring one eye, the Eugenie hat was widely copied.

▲ Joan Crawford wearing the "Letty Lynton" dress, which spawned a thousand copies.

◄ In the hands of British stars like Gertrude Lawrence and Ivor Novello, fashion on the musical stage was as glamorous and up-to-date as on the screen.

► Bette Davis, a liberated woman in a male dominated industry, specialized in difficult and powerful roles, setting a new standard for women on the big screen. On-screen and off, she personified a slightly aloof elegance. Inset: style was not restricted to the women: Clark Gable, the unchallenged king of Hollywood, was the fashion yardstick for men all over the world.

▲Marlene Dietrich favored a personal style of casual tailoring, whether she wore skirts or, a little uncommon for the time, slacks.

◄ Screen goddess Greta Garbo wears the Eugenie hat designed for her by Adrian for the movie *Camille* (1936).

In 1932, a dress that Adrian designed for Joan Crawford proved so popular that Macy's department store in New York reported selling over half a million dresses in similar styles. This was the "Letty Lynton dress": a wide-shouldered, white organdy dress with ruffled sleeves, extended shoulders, and a nipped-in waist.

Although the influential fashion trade paper *Women's Wear Daily* had reported a year earlier that French designers were exaggerating the widths of shoulders with new cuts, revers, and capelets, Adrian's Letty Lynton dress accelerated the conversion to the wide-shouldered style. The optical illusion this created, of narrower waists and hips, emphasized a woman's natural shape and directed attention down to shapely legs and ankles.

Each of the stars had their own look, created for them by their designers. Greta Garbo, for instance, was known for her pageboy hairstyles, tailored suits, and, in particular, her belted trench coat worn with dark glasses, a beret, or a floppy-brimmed hat.

The Blonde Bombshell

Blonde hair was greatly admired, much sought after, and easily acquired. Peroxide was brushed on the hair, usually with a toothbrush, and reapplied until the desired shade was achieved. Many of the starlets in Hollywood were groomed

▲Jean Harlow, "the Blonde Bombshell," in 1933. The halter-neck, bias-cut silk, and exaggerated fur trimmings are all intended to underscore her famous sex appeal.

to be blondes, and the ultimate in blondness was platinum blonde. Jean Harlow, the most famous of them all, was usually featured in her films slinking about in satin, bias-cut halter-neck gowns. In her short career, "the Blonde Bombshell" inspired thousands, if not millions, of women to bleach their hair, with varying degrees of success.

For millions of movie fans, glamour meant Marlene Dietrich. Often cast as a sophisticated, somewhat mysterious femme fatale, Dietrich wore clothes that were dressy but not fussy, tailored but never too masculine. Despite the new skirt lengths, Dietrich somehow always managed to show off her elegant and shapely legs. And while Mae West displayed her hourglass figure in tight-fitting floor-length dresses, it was Joan Crawford who gave the second half of the decade another universal fashion: the bright red, cupid's-bow mouth.

Hollywood in Fashion

The looks and clothes of the Hollywood stars were not the only thing that women copied. The type of women the actresses portrayed also had their effect on women's behavior, language, and gestures. The restless, flighty flappers of the 1920s were replaced by a new "modern" type of woman: glamorous, articulate, and independent—the perfect match for their "tough guy" partners.

But Hollywood did not restrict itself to glamour. It also spawned crazes for pseudo-historical fashions like the small, round, open-weave Juliet caps and long velvet dresses worn by Norma Shearer in *Romeo and Juliet* or boater hats with ribbons as worn by Katharine Hepburn in *Little Women*. None of the costumes in these films were historically accurate, however, since they were always modified to meet with star approval and suit contemporary tastes.

But just when it seemed that Hollywood designers could get away with anything, the 1934 Hays Code of censorship was imposed. In addition to banning certain language, subjects, and behavior from the screen, the Hays Code meant that low-cut or revealing dresses were banned. Filmmakers worked around the restrictions and devised new situations for their characters, while the designers cut away at dresses to reveal a new, "safe" area of women's bodies—their backs.

The impact of Hollywood was such that magazines like *Vogue* began asking whether Paris or Hollywood was creating the new fashions. In fact, it was more of a swapping of ideas. European designers Marcel Rochas, Alix, Edward Molyneux, Jean Patou, and Jeanne Lanvin all traveled to California to design for films, and the film designers also made trips to Europe, researching material for their creations. Furthermore, the stars themselves spent their new fortunes traveling to Europe to be dressed.

In 1935, Elsa Schiaparelli opened a boutique in Place Vendôme in Paris—the first of its kind and the model nearly all couturiers would follow in the future. Schiaparelli's first private customer was Anita Loos, author of *Gentlemen Prefer Blondes*, and throughout the decade, she went on to dress a galaxy of stars, among them Marlene Dietrich, Claudette Colbert, Norma Shearer, and Gloria Swanson.

Art Deco: Themes and Machines

Streamline Style

Art Deco was a style that drew on the art of different cultures for its motifs. In the 1920s, elements of the style had been taken from African and pre-Columbian art, and after the discovery in 1922 of Tutankhamen's tomb, Egyptian themes became hugely popular. Alongside motifs of fountains, gazelles, hunting dogs, and zebras, these elements were incorporated into fabric designs and pieces of jewelry.

By the 1930s, the hallmark of the Art Deco style was its geometry, largely derived from the Cubist movement in art. All the motifs, from flowers and animals to the human figure, became angular, but the most popular subjects were the hard-edged forms of zigzags, electric flashes, and sun-ray motifs. The geometric shapes of Art Deco lent themselves perfectly to strong colors and contrasts, with red, black, white, and silver being one of the most fashionable color combinations.

The greatest stylistic innovation of the Depression era, and an important aspect of Art Deco, was streamlining. Speed was one of the marvels of the modern age, and the shapes and lines dictated by aerodynamics were incorporated into the work of many designers. In America, the style was embraced by a wave of European designers who came to the United States to escape the rise of Fascism and the imminent war in Europe. But the prophet of streamlining was industrial designer Norman Bel Geddes. Many of Bel Geddes's ideas were visionary rather than practical, but through his efforts, streamlining became the accepted style. It also came to be seen as a symbol of optimism and promise for the future, suggesting a nation moving forward out of the Depression to become the powerhouse of the new machine age.

Manhattan Skyline

The best examples of the Art Deco style are to be found in the design of skyscrapers. Skyscrapers were born of the problems of constructing buildings in the restricted spaces of cities like Chicago and New York, but since they quickly became potent symbols of commercial power, many were built in towns and cities where building space was not in particularly short supply.

▲The Chrysler Building, New York: a towering monument to the success of the Chrysler Motor Corporation.

►The folds of this evening gown by Alix are closely modeled on the flowing drapery of the ancient Greek sculpture "Winged Victory."

On the left is a charming red dress with the right kind of presence for almost any daytime occasion. It has uncommon raglan sleeves, and slanting seams on bodice and skirt broken by tabs. The coat has a very good line. It would be attractive in a green diagonally woven fabric with flat sleek fur. Notice the slightly bloused top which is so good for too wide hips, the pretty cuffs and collar. The little red jacket made in a heavyweight cloth is a charming substitute for the short fur coat for warmer weather. It has a pretty scalloped seam effect making pockets beneath the belt.

he new Line Slants

▲Traveling clothes of 1932 from *Woman's Journal.* The short red jacket in heavyweight cloth offers the freedom of movement needed for driving, while the other outfits are perhaps more suitable for the passenger seat or the railroad car.

The most famous of all the skyscrapers built in the 1930s are in New York City. Begun in 1931, Rockefeller Center is a complex of offices, shops, restaurants, and theaters that included the RKO Roxy movie theater and Radio City Music Hall. The Empire State Building of 1931 rises 102 stories above the city and included, at its summit, a mooring for airships. Unfortunately, the updrafts and currents created by neighboring tall buildings made the use of airships in cities impossible.

The best example of the Art Deco skyscraper is the 1930 Chrysler Building. Its overall shape is a ziggurat, or stepped pyramid, topped by a tower and spire with sculpted decorations inspired by automobile parts like radiator grilles and hubcaps. The building not only suggests the wealth of the Chrysler Corporation but, in its decoration, also recalls the Chrysler car.

Material Advances

Not only were the headquarters and factories of the manufacturing giants built in the new style but so were small gas stations, bars, restaurants, and movie houses. These buildings used modern and inexpensive materials: enamels, plastics, wood, and aluminum could all be produced as prefabricated units. The styles and materials of streamlining, representing everything that was forward-looking, modern, clean, and efficient, proved themselves flexible enough for use not only on the super-sleek transcontinental trains and skyscrapers but for a wide range of low-cost, mass-produced consumer items like kitchen appliances, radios, and even fashion accessories.

The belief that something inexpensive could also be fashionable first appears with Art Deco. The fashion of earlier decades had been more or less confined to the wealthy, who were happy to pay for expensive materials and exclusive designs. Gabrielle (Coco) Chanel captured the new spirit in a range of clothes designed on simple lines in inexpensive fabrics like cotton, and her designs could be easily copied by the home dressmaker. Chanel also helped to popularize costume jewelry made of inexpensive materials like plastic.

◀ This smart red necklace is made of Bakelite. This new plastic, made by Dr. Leo Baekeland, a Belgian chemist, became one of the wonder substances of the decade and was used for everything from jewelry to telephones.

▲The Greyhound bus was another triumph of streamlining, its long, lean lines suggesting speed and comfort.

◀ This enamel and white-metal watch, from the middle of the decade, has the classic stepped pyramid design so typical of Art Deco.

▲Bakelite, this time colored to look like ivory, was used for this radio, made by the Italian firm Ducati.

▲The Phantom Corsair, designed by Rust Heinz in 1937. A styling exercise for the "car of the future," it looks some twenty years ahead of its time.

▲A blue-and-white-striped suit of 1936 shows many Art Deco influences in its pattern, cut, and detailing.

Plastic became chic simply because it was a novelty, but it was also cheap enough to be available to all—not just the better off—and versatile enough to mimic ivory, ebony, jade, or coral. Fashion could now be mass-produced, and the make-believe glamour of the movies was within the reach of everyone who aspired to it.

New Materials: Revealing the Body Beautiful

From Silk to Rayon

Not only did the clothes that women wore in the 1930s become more womanly, women also wore fewer of them. The new curvy shape that women sought was enhanced by a variety of fabrics, some old and some new, that could be cut and draped to show off the wearer's body.

In addition to the various silks, wools, and linens designers had always used, they now had at their disposal a whole range of synthetic materials. Since these new fabrics could be produced inexpensively, they were often used for mass-produced clothing. Some designers, however—notably Elsa Schiaparelli and Victor Stiebel— incorporated synthetic materials into their haute couture range.

Since the late nineteenth century, the search for synthetic substitutes for natural materials had concentrated on silk. Silk was the most expensive raw material because it was the hardest to produce: the mulberry tree on which the silkworms feed will grow only in certain climates. Experiments in the last years of the nineteenth century led to the development of artificial silk, later called rayon, which was made of wood cellulose treated with chemicals to produce long, silk-like threads. The new fiber, once woven into cloth, produced a fabric that not only draped well but also had a high absorbency, which meant it could be dyed easily.

Looking and feeling like silk, rayon was used for lingerie at the less expensive end of the market, and since it was also washable, a whole range of ready-to-wear, crease-resistant dresses became available, in colors from the palest pastels to the deepest blues.

"I never buy *handled* hosiery!"

["CELLOPHANE" WRAP PREVENTS DAMAGE—SAVES YOU MONEY]

HEAVEN protect silk stockings from the careless hands of shoppers and clerks! One sharp fingernail or one rough finger can weaken fragile silk threads in less time than you can say "Darn!" Avoid this by getting hosiery in neat Cellophane packets that protect against handling. You'll also find silk lingerie in Cellophane transparent wrapping, all beautifully laundered and ready to wear. No woman wants to buy lingerie that's been pawed over by strange hands. The Cellophane wrap keeps it spotlessly clean. E. I. du Pont de Nemours & Co., Inc., "Cellophane" Division, Wilmington, Del.

Cellophane
THE DU PONT CELLULOSE FILM

DU PONT

▲This woman is delighted that her silk stockings are protected by their new cellophane packaging, but by the end of the decade, the stockings themselves would probably be made of an artificial material.

▶The secret of this simple dress worn by screen star Gloria Swanson is in the figure-hugging drape. The outfit is set off by a stunning selection of jewelry based on ethnic designs.

▲The Surrealists seem to have taken over this particular fashion shoot, which promotes a white rayon suit from Dorville, dating from 1938.

▲Beachwear styles of 1935 in Krepe-Tex from the American Charnaux Company, promising fit "as never before."

Rayon was also widely used for stockings, but in 1939 it would be replaced by a new fabric, nylon. Nylon was the result of a research program begun in 1927 by Wallace H. Caruthers at the Du Pont Company in Delaware. In 1938, Du Pont produced nylon commercially and in the following year successfully tested it in knitted hosiery. By the end of the decade, nylon stockings had replaced the often shiny and poorly fitting rayon ones.

Fabrics Galore

Rayon and nylon are perhaps the two most familiar synthetic fabrics from a whole host of intriguingly named materials. We are also familiar with cellophane, but we don't usually associate it with fashion. Yet it was out of this material that Alix created an evening dress likened to the wing case of a shiny black beetle. Victor Stiebel also used cellophane, in conjunction with white taffeta, in an accordion-pleated gown modeled in *Vogue* in 1936 by Vivien Leigh.

Metallic fabrics were also popular. Lamé is the name given to fabrics woven with flat metallic threads, immensely popular for evening wear. Sequins and beads made from colored plastics and glass also swathed women's bodies in shimmering light effects.

Rhodophane, a less well known fabric developed in the 1920s by the French company Colcombet, was a glass-like fabric made from a mixture of cellophane and other synthetics. It was versatile enough to look either like clear glass or a gauzy cobweb. Despite its fragile appearance, Rhodophane was used

▶Artificial crepe is the material for this cinema frock. Clearly, a new kind of social occasion demanded a whole new style of garment and a new fabric.

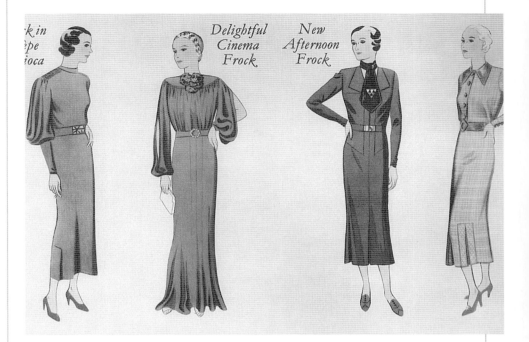

k in epe ioca

Delightful Cinema Frock.

New Afternoon Frock.

by Schiaparelli for a variety of dresses and accessories, including handbags and even shoes.

The new synthetic materials were not just confined to evening wear and lingerie. They also gave a boost to accessories and leisure wear. Elastic yarns made of rubber combined with silk, cotton, or rayon produced a fabric that, since it clung to the body and kept its shape when wet, was ideal for swimwear. Plastic materials could be molded and colored to create jewelry, handbag frames, belt buckles, and sunglasses. Plastic zippers, in matching or contrasting colors, were pioneered by Schiaparelli, first in sportswear and later on in evening dresses.

◀ The typical Art Deco handbag that completes actress Myrna Loy's elegant outfit owes its neat, flat shape and shiny surface to the new materials.

Halter Necks and Bias Cuts

Madame Vionnet Cuts It

In the 1920s, the well-known couturier Madame Madeleine Vionnet had devised a method of cutting fabric called "bias cutting." This involved cutting across the grain of the fabric and had two distinct **advantages** over ordinary cutting techniques, despite the fact that it required a greater width of material. First, when a dress was made up of bias-cut pieces, the fabric draped in sinuous folds and clung to the wearer's body where it touched. Second, the dress would stretch sufficiently to allow the wearer to put it on over her head or simply step into it, without the need for any side, back, or front openings.

Using bias-cutting techniques, designers could produce gowns in silk, satin, chiffon, and crepe that would cling around the bosom, waist, and hips and flare out from the thighs into an elegant sweep of skirt. The bias-cutting technique continued into the thirties, but the evening dresses now had an added new element: they were backless. Some dresses were held up by narrow shoulder straps, while others had halter necks, where the high panel of the front was tied around the back of the neck, leaving the back and shoulders completely exposed.

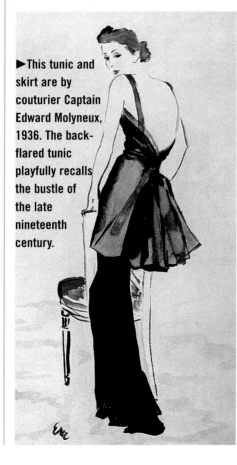

►This tunic and skirt are by couturier Captain Edward Molyneux, 1936. The back-flared tunic playfully recalls the bustle of the late nineteenth century.

Hollywood's Back Plunge

It has been argued that the fashion for plunging backs came out of Hollywood's ban on low necklines, but it is also likely that the bare-backed style was influenced by the increasing fashion for sunbathing and swimwear designs cut low at the back to allow maximum tanning.

Whatever its origins, the new fashion for evening dresses was certainly elegant. In order to attract even more attention to the back, there was a vogue for wearing strings of beads or pearls swinging down the

►A flowing georgette evening gown of 1930, with full scarf and trimmed skirt. A single string of pearls hangs from the back of the model's neck.

▲ "The interest begins at the top" in this selection of evening gowns from 1932. Of particular interest are the varying treatments of sleeves and shoulder straps. From the waist down, things are a little more standardized.

▲ Paris designs for winter 1935, with low backs, bias cuts, and diagonal seams.

◄ Designs from 1936 by (left) Lucien Lelong and (right) Jean Patou. The Lelong design twists mulberry and emerald ribbons into a column that extends down the spine; Patou slashes the front of the predominantly black/brown dress to reveal a rainbow of colors beneath.

back and artificial flowers pinned at the base of the spine. Elsa Schiaparelli went so far as to design a backless dress with a bustle that jutted out like a shelf.

Satins and Furs

To complement the sweep of the skirt, many women carried large, brightly colored chiffon handkerchiefs. Also popular for evening wear were fox furs. Entire animals—or, better still, two animals—were draped over bare shoulders. The most sought-after furs were those of the silver fox, but ultra-fashionable women adopted white fox capes for evening wear

For day wear, bias-cut skirts that flared from the hips lent themselves to a new fashion for stripes and checks on the bias. For evenings, heavy crepes and dull satins gave flowing, folding, and draping dresses their most statuesque qualities. The greatest draper and molder of jersey, silk, and wool was Alix Barton, later known as Madame Grès, who opened her own fashion house in Paris in 1934. With great patience and skill, Alix pleated fabrics into precise, elegant, and simple shapes that resembled Greek sculptures.

▶ Classic design from Alix (Madame Grès) in 1937. It may not be surprising to learn that her early ambition was to be a sculptor.

▲The new, more revealing dresses called for underwear that was itself more brief and that, while being less restrictive, could offer firm control. Panty girdles in Lastex from the Kestos Company of America solved the problem.

◀ This figure-hugging evening dress by Schiaparelli, also from 1937, is worn with laced ballerina shoes.

Schiaparelli and the Surrealists

Objects and Illusions

Surrealism was one of the major international art movements of the thirties. Initiated in the 1920s by André Breton—who wrote its manifesto—and drawing on the Dada movement, dreams, and Freudian analysis, Surrealism was initially a literary movement involving writers like Louis Aragon, Jean Cocteau, and Paul Eluard but soon moved on to embrace the visual. The Surrealists were fascinated by objects removed from their usual setting and seen in some new, often bizarre context. This disruption in the traditional role, scale, and association was intended to shock the viewer and produce a completely new interpretation of the scene. There was no single Surrealist style. Some paintings are eerie landscapes inhabited by objects that are not identifiable from the conscious world, while others, like Dalí's "dreamscapes," place distorted familiar objects into strange locations.

Influential on art and literature, Surrealism also began to affect fashion. And not only in the way that fashion was presented—in illustration, photography and window displays—but in the clothes themselves.

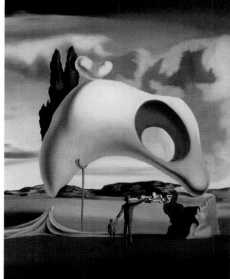

▲ *Atavistic Relics After Rain*, 1934, by arch-Surrealist Salvador Dalí.

▶A relatively restrained Schiaparelli evening coat in tweed, from 1936. The revers are lavishly beaded for contrast, and the headdress shows Asian influences.

▲A feather motif comes into its own in this gown.

Mutton Chops and Slippers

The designer most influenced by Surrealism was Italian Elsa Schiaparelli. Her first commercially successful design, around 1926, was for a trompe l'oeil ("fool the eye") sweater. A simple black wool sweater with a white butterfly bow knitted in at the neck, its instant success enabled Schiaparelli to establish a business in Paris concentrating on sportswear, tailored clothes, and evening wear. But Schiaparelli liked nothing better than to amuse, either through wit or shock tactics, and like her Surrealist friends, she was also fond of displacing elements, using tweed for evening clothes and burlap for day dresses.

The classic exercise in Surrealist fashion displacement was the Shoe Hat, the product of a collaboration between Schiaparelli and Salvador Dalí. In 1932, Dalí had posed for a photograph wearing his wife, Gala's, slipper on his head, and in 1937, he designed the now famous Shoe Hat for Schiaparelli. In a true Surrealist cycle of events, Dalí then photographed Gala wearing the Shoe Hat, dressed in a suit with lips for pockets. Other Dalí-Schiaparelli creations included the Ice-Cream Cone Hat and the Mutton-Chop Hat, which perfectly matched a suit embroidered with cutlet motifs.

◄ Schiaparelli's famous tear dress, with matching cape, from 1938 (*see page 51*).

▲Schiaparelli's perfume "Shocking" was thought to be very French, despite the bottle being modeled on all-American Mae West.

▲The famous fingernail gloves, paired with a three-quarter-length black evening dress.

Fabric designs by Christian Berard and Jean Cocteau were complemented by a range of bizarre accessories: clear plastic necklaces decorated with colored metal insects that appear to crawl directly on the wearer's neck; handbags that look like bird cages; ceramic vegetables and aspirins as necklaces (designed in conjunction with poet Louis Aragon); glowing brooches and buttons shaped like paperweights or grasshoppers.

Also imaginative and inventive was Schiaparelli's use of zippers, which she incorporated into the designs of garments. A simple dress with a zipper in a

SCIAPARELLI acaba de lanzar estos dos modelos de sombreros inspirados en los de los monos de circo.

▲ Two more Schiaparelli creations from 1938. Although they somewhat resemble women's riding hats, these are definitely hats-about-town.

◀ Schiaparelli creations in wool for daytime wear, 1938. The fabrics are jersey and tweed, and the pinched waists are beltless.

contrasting color may not seem outrageous now, but at the time, it was completely new.

A Shocking Experience

Schiaparelli's perfumes also bore the stamp of Surrealism. She marketed two fragrances in the thirties, named—thanks to her preference for names beginning with her own initial—Shocking and Sleeping. The hourglass-shaped bottle for Shocking was designed by Surrealist artist Leonor Fini and based on the silhouette of Hollywood actress Mae West, who had sent Schiaparelli a life-size plaster caste of herself in the pose of Venus de Milo as a model for the dresses she had ordered to wear in her film *Sapphire Sal*. The bottle for Sleeping took the form of a candlestick, a reference to the world of dreams, always a potent source of Surrealist imagery.

Although Schiaparelli had been "shocking" her clients throughout the decade, her moment of triumph came in the 1937–1938 season. Returning to trompe l'oeil effects, she produced a jacket, inspired by Jean Cocteau, which had a pair of clasped hands embroidered at the waist and a woman's hair, suggested by gold bugle beading, flowing down one sleeve.

The Harlequin Collection produced the Domino motif hat, while the Circus Collection showed the words "Beware of Fresh Paint" on the back of a dress as well as hats named Chicken-in-a-Basket, Quill-Pen, and Ink-Well. Collaborating with Dalí, she created the Lobster Dress: a giant pink lobster surrounded by sprigs of parsley printed onto an organdy dress. Dalí also helped design the fabric for Schiaparelli's Tear Dress and matching cape. An evening gown to be worn at the most formal of functions, it appears to have been torn repeatedly. And since the cape (see p 49) did, in fact, have real tears in it, the outfit—even when brand new—looked like it had already been ruined.

Just as Surrealist artists played games with people's expectations of art, Schiaparelli transformed clothing—the greatest of all the illusionistic devices—by allowing the unexpected to replace convention.

Shaping Up: Health and Fitness

Sport for All

During the thirties, physical activity and sun worshiping assumed cult proportions. One of the manifestations was the Women's League of Health and Beauty, founded in Britain by Prunella Stack in 1930. In their uniform of brief, black satin shorts and sleeveless white satin blouses, thousands of league members gave public demonstrations of physical fitness, based on the principle that a trained body was the secret to a simple but happy life.

All over England and continental Europe, naturist clubs and health and sports societies were formed to pay homage to the body beautiful. Nudism and hiking had come from Germany, and all through the thirties, Austria and Germany were fashionable European holiday destinations. The effect on fashion was a trend toward Tyrolean peasant dirndl skirts, shorts, and feathered hats, as youngsters and adults alike joined hiking clubs.

People were so obsessed with keeping fit that a strike by French taxi drivers in 1936 started a craze for bicycling. Naturally, special cycling suits were a must!

Even if she didn't take part in any sporting activity but was content to watch, the fashion-conscious woman could wear what the fashion magazines called "spectator-sports clothes." For spring and autumn, these were skirt-suits and coats in tweeds and checked wools, while in summer, navy blue jackets and white skirts were appropriate wear for watching tennis or polo.

The navy-blue-and-white combination was also popular wear on cruise ships or at holiday resorts. To emphasize a nautical look, motifs like anchors and ship's wheels were embroidered on pockets and lapels.

MOTORING AND SPORTS WEAR.

MAN-TAILORED COSTUME.
Obtainable in a variety of the newest styles and materials. To order. From £7 7 0

FOR MOTORING.
In natural Chamois, with Sleeves.
£2 12 6

LEATHER AND SUEDE SPORTS JACKET.
In fine quality.
Colours : Brown or Tan shades.
From £3 13 6

TWEED SKIRTS.
To order 63/-

A PRACTICAL MOTOR COAT.
Made of Semi-chrome Leather and lined Tweed.
Obtainable in chocolate or tan shades.

SLEEVELESS CHAMOIS LEATHER WAISTCOAT.
For Hunting or Sports wear.

▲Motoring and sportswear for the women of 1938. The cut echoes the forms of evening wear, although in more robust materials—suede, leather, and tweed predominate, and neckties and scarves are popular.

▲The fashionable female cyclist opted for culottes or somewhat elongated "shorts."

ON THE CRUISE
AND AFTER

A suit like this will be useful as a deck suit on the cruise and to wear in town later. The suit is in red Royalist silk edged with white. The dress is in two parts—blouse and skirt. You wear a matching blouse or a sports shirt in white Viyella. There's the biggest selection of these in plain colours and jolly stripes, ready to wear and priced from 6/6. Ask to see them at your nearest shop.

▲This feature from *What to Wear and How to Make It* magazine shows red, navy and white cruisewear in a casual style.

Freedom of Movement

With the increased popularity of active sports, designers of sportswear now had to address the functional needs of the sports rather than simply altering existing day-wear styles, while at the same time maintaining a fashionable silhouette. Active sportswear had to allow for maximum movement. Skating skirts were now shorter than they had ever been, well above the knee and pleated or flared for movement and an eye-catching line. The sport itself was given a boost by the champion skater-turned-Hollywood-star Sonja Henie, who skated through her films in a variety of lavish one-piece skating dresses.

As winter sports grew in popularity, a skiing vacation became an annual event for those who could afford it. Fashionable ski outfits consisted of matching jackets and pants that were worn tucked into lace-up ski boots and finished off with a weatherproof cap.

►Sonja Henie's films usually featured balletic skating sequences. *Sun Valley Serenade,* shown here, could be mistaken for *Swan Lake.*

Fun in the Sun

As the "fun-in-the-sun" mentality encouraged a heightened body consciousness, men's and women's sportswear became more and more revealing.

Standard tennis wear for men had been long white flannel pants, with the cuffs turned up for play, white shirts with rolled-up sleeves, white socks, and white, crepe-soled shoes. Fashion-conscious players in the thirties, however, started to opt for one of French tennis star René Lacoste's short-sleeved shirts, with a small collar, buttons, and the famous alligator emblem on the chest. Although some amateur players, finding the long flannels too hot and uncomfortable, switched to shorts, professional players still played in long pants until the 1932 Men's National Tennis Championships at Forest Hills, New York, when Bunny Austin dared to wear shorts.

Bare legs for women on the tennis courts was a trend started in 1928 by the Spanish player Lili de Alvarez, who played in a just-below-the-knee culotte dress designed by Schiaparelli. Total freedom of movement came in 1933, when Alice Marble wore shorts at the Wimbledon championships.

Bare on the Beach

Designers were also cutting away at swimwear. In the 1920s, men had worn one-piece swimsuits that covered their chests. Gentlemen who bared their chests in public were not just considered disrespectful, they risked being arrested. By 1932, men at private beach resorts began to follow the European lead of swimming

▲Elastic waistbands for tennis pants and shorts meant goodbye to suspenders forever. These chain-store styles for men and women date from 1934.

▲The military influence, on both fabric and cut, is unmistakable in this weekend casual wear from France, 1939.

Top tennis star Bunny Austin's athletic prowess was obviously given a boost by the freedom offered by the new designs in men's shorts.

without shirts. Driven by the craze for suntans, the most popular swimsuits for men and women were those that offered maximum body exposure. Once men had cast off their shirts, designers set to work on the trunks: legs were cut higher and new knitted fabrics like Lastex promised a figure-hugging fit. Fashion offered a variety of solutions to the problems posed by the laws governing decency on public beaches. The Jantzen Topper model of 1934 had a zipper waist that allowed for the attachment of a swim shirt when decorum ruled. But by 1935, attitudes had changed sufficiently to allow men to swim in trunks alone at most public beaches.

Women bathers, in their pursuit of greater freedom and maximum exposure, eventually abandoned the yards of over-skirts and shirts of the earlier styles and adopted a one- or two-piece swimsuit based on the male prototype.

►Swimming costumes for men from the renowned Jantzen label. These novel and ever more brief designs were only made possible by the new stretch fabrics.

Ai
Signori piace
lo "Jantzen,,

AI SIGNORI PIACE LO STIL BUONO . . . se pratico e combinat col conforto. Lo Jantzen piace perch ad un aspetto elegante unisce la massim libertà nel nuotare. Lavorato a magli strette con lana fortissima di fibra lunga, l Jantzen si adatta al vostro corpo perfetta mente, senza una piega! Data la sua str ordinaria elasticità lo Jantzen mantier sempre la sua forma elegante.

Sono illustrati il "Twosome,, e "Speed-Suit,,. Li troverete senza bottoni con bottoni infragibili di gomma. Come tutti Jantzen sono lavorati a maglie strette con lai fortissima di fibra lunga. Esaminate i modelli vivaci colori per Signori, Signore e fanciulli ne principali negozi. Colori resistenti perché già ti nel filato. Il vostro peso indica la misura del costum Badate alla marca di fabbrica "Bagnante ros che si tuffa,,, che ogni vero Jantzen deve portar

Chiedete al vostro fornitore il prospetto con la tavola dei colori armonizzanti o scrivete direttamente all' ITALO AMERICAN TRADING COMPANY, VIA LUIGI CALA-MATTA 16, ROMA (126).

Jantzen
Il costume che vi dà libertà nel nuotare
MADE IN AMERICA

The End of the Rainbow

The Gathering Storm

By 1936, the worst years of the Depression were over and the number of unemployed people was beginning to fall. But it was also the year that the political sky grew darker. The Spanish Civil War, which broke out in July, was seen by many as the showdown between the political left and right in Europe.

When the Germans bombed the Basque town of Guernica, almost wiping out the entire population, the world was outraged. Pablo Picasso's famous painting *Guernica* (see p 25), which commemorated the event, went on tour throughout Europe in an effort to raise people's consciousness about the war. Despite the efforts of the many Europeans and Americans who joined the International Brigade to fight on the Republican side, it was soon clear that Franco and his German and Italian allies would win. Greatly encouraged by their exploits in Spain, Hitler and Mussolini began building up their own forces.

War was not confined to Europe, however. In the same year, Japan invaded China and seized Beijing and Shanghai, forcing the government to move to Hankow and uniting Chiang Kai-shek with the Chinese Communist forces led by Mao Zedong and Zhou Enlai. It was only a matter of time before the storm broke over the world.

A Rodex Model

▶"The aristocrat of coats for half a century" was the proud slogan of Rodex, makers of coats in fine tweed. These coats were exported all over the world, their status boosted by the guarantee that "Rodex coats conform to the best English traditions and are made exclusively by British people."

▲Color makes a comeback in these outdoor outfits by Margaret Barry, Eva Lutyens, and W. W. Reville-Terry.

◄ ▲These two typical suits of 1938, with broader shoulders and boxy jackets, were perhaps a foretaste of the military styles of the war years. Hats and button details, however, show these designs to be rooted firmly in the prewar era.

Gearing Up

Fashion designers responded to and reflected the prevailing mood of these troubled years. Daytime fashion became more severe and militarily inspired, with square, epauletted shoulders, frog fastenings, feathered hats, gauntlet gloves, and sensible, low-heeled shoes. Like soldiers, women were expected to be meticulously groomed and to pay attention to every tiny detail.

By 1938, it was clear that war was not far off. That season's designs were seen by *Vogue* as being useful "factory" looks. Hair was pinned up safely and hidden under scarves, suits were broader shouldered, and skirts were a little more skimpy, using less fabric. In contrast, evening dresses cast a nostalgic look back at a more romantic and peaceful past with crinolines (stiff underskirts), tight waists, and frills.

A year later, Europe was engulfed by war—but not before a whole new industry of ready-to-wear clothing had been established, catering to the needs and desires of people who wanted moderately priced, fashionable clothes. Thousands of Europeans fled the oppressive regimes in their homelands to seek refuge in Britain and America, among them many skilled tailors, seamstresses, and dressmakers, who brought not only their labor but a sense

►Suitcase labels from romantic places: in this case, the Italian lakes.

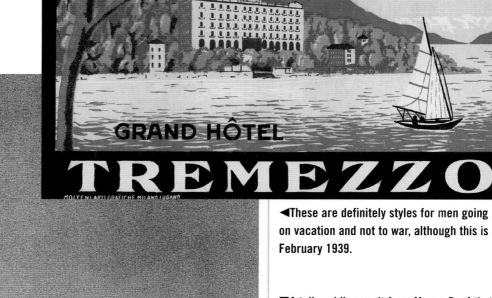

◄These are definitely styles for men going on vacation and not to war, although this is February 1939.

▼A tailored linen suit from Maggy Rouf that looks forward to the styles and cuts of the following decade. The flower-decked Suzy hat claims inspiration from French Impressionist painter Claude Monet.

of continental style that had been lacking in some areas of British and American design.

In 1939, European couturiers went to war with clothes that were practical and, in most cases, the last they would design until peace was restored. They produced shirtwaist dresses and simple suits that would not date, while sweaters and pants became acceptable fashion wear. Makeup artists like Helena Rubenstein and Cyclax responded with spiritedly named lipsticks like Regimental Red and Auxilliary Red. The ever resourceful Schiaparelli produced designs in Maginot Line Blue and Foreign Legion Red before embarking on a lecture tour of the United States, where she was to spend most of the war years.

One trend that emerged very briefly in the Paris collections of 1939, only to disappear almost immediately, was the sharply defined waist. In contrast to her earlier styles, Coco Chanel showed tight-waisted, full-skirted dresses, while Mainbocher displayed full-skirted dirndls. Not until Christian Dior's New Look in 1947— the first postwar fashion to have a strong impact—would slim waists again be featured so strongly.

But for the time being at least, there were to be no more escapist follies or fashion fantasies. All over the world, practical fashions were in style.

▶Anticipating the shape of the Dior "New Look," with its emphasis on the nipped-in waist, Mainbocher's 1939 collection can also be seen as pointing the way to the style of the forties.

Chronology

News

1930 Parliamentary democracy comes to an end in Germany.

1931 Japanese invade Manchuria.
Proclamation of Republic in Spain.

1932 Franklin Delano Roosevelt elected president of the United States.

1933 Hitler becomes Chancellor of Germany.
Roosevelt announces New Deal.
Prohibition repealed.
Reichstag fire.

1934 "Night of the Long Knives".
Nazi purge in Germany.
The Japanese make Henry Pu-yi, last emperor of China, puppet ruler of Manchukuo (Manchuria).

1935 Germany repudiates military provisions of Versailles Treaty.
Nuremberg laws deprive Jews of rights in Germany.
Mussolini invades Abyssinia (modern-day Ethiopia).

1936 Death of King George V.
Abdication of Edward VIII.
Rebellion brings in Spanish Army.
Spanish Civil War begins.
Rome–Berlin Axis proclaimed by Mussolini.

1937 German airforce bombs Basque town of Guernica, Spain.
Rioting in Czech Sudetenland.
Japanese seize Shanghai and Beijing.

1938 Nazi Germany annexes Austria.
Chamberlain meets Hitler at Munich.

1939 Germany invades Czechoslovakia.
Italy invades Albania.
Britain, France, Australia, and New Zealand declare war on Germany.
Russia invades Poland and Finland.

Events

Amy Johnson flies solo to Australia.
Youth Hostels Association formed.
Chrysler Building in NYC completed; 1,046 feet high.

Empire State Building in NYC completed; 1,250 feet high.

Great Hunger March of unemployed to London.
Campbell drives racing car Bluebird at 235 mph.
George Washington Bridge over the Hudson River opened.

Polythene first made.

Ocean liner *Queen Mary* launched.
Popular song: *Smoke Gets in Your Eyes.*

Silver Jubilee of George V and Queen Mary.
Radar invented.
Mickey Mouse appears in color.

Olympic Games in Berlin.
Exhibition of Surrealist art in London. Dalí attends wearing deep-sea diving suit.
Margaret Mitchell publishes best-selling novel *Gone with the Wind.*

First full-length Disney cartoon: *Snow White and the Seven Dwarfs.*
Picasso paints *Guernica.*
Golden Gate Bridge, San Francisco completed.
Duke of Windsor marries Wallis Simpson.

Chaplin's *Modern Times* is released.
George Biro makes first practical ballpoint pen.

Vivien Leigh and Clark Gable star in *Gone with the Wind.*
German battleship *Bismarck* launched.
John Steinbeck publishes *The Grapes of Wrath.*

Fashion

Women's League of Health and Beauty formed in Britain.

Chanel shows collection of 35 cotton evening dresses.
Mainbocher is first American designer to open a Paris salon.

Schiaparelli introduces a bustle to her backless evening gowns.
Margaret Rose dresses made popular for children by Princess Margaret in England.
Adrian designs Letty Lynton dress for Joan Crawford movie.

Garbo stars in *Grand Hotel*; Mae West in *She Done Him Wrong.*
René Lacoste introduces short-sleeved tennis shirt.
Influence of Hollywood at its highest.

Molyneux designs trousseau for Princess Marina.
Tyrolean look popular.
Alix (Madame Grès) opens Paris salon.

Schiaparelli opens her boutique in Paris.
Popular color in Britain is Jubilee Blue.

Steibel creates Cellophane and taffeta dress.
Schiaparelli designs clothes and accessories in Rhodophane.
Surrealist influence on fashion design and illustration at its height.

Schiaparelli launches fragrance "Shocking" in Mae West inspired bottle.
Italian shoe designer Ferragamo introduces the wedge heel.
Dali and Schiaparelli produce the Shoe-Hat.

Schiaparelli launches fragrance "Sleeping".
Ferragamo develops the platform-soled shoe.

Sweaters and trousers appear in *Vogue.*
Paris shows tight-waisted dresses, a prelude to the postwar New Look.
Schiaparelli and Mainbocher leave Paris for the United States.

Glossary

Adrian (Gilbert Adrian) (1903–59)
American designer of stage costumes for Broadway shows until 1925, when he moved to Hollywood to make clothes for Rudolph Valentino. After working with Cecile B. De Mille, Adrian moved to MGM, where he designed costumes for Greta Garbo, Joan Crawford, Jean Harlow, and Norma Shearer.

Alix (Madame Alix Grès) (1910–93) French designer Grès opened her first fashion house in 1934 as Alix Barton. She was renowned for her ability to drape and mold silks and jerseys until they resembled the flutes of classical columns.

Antoine (1884–1976) Polish-born hairdresser Antoine ran a beauty practice in Saks Fifth Avenue, New York, from 1925 to 1939. He created the popular Shingle Cut of the late 1920s, and designed the upswept hairstyles of the thirties and was responsible for the creation of Greta Garbo's long bob and Claudette Colbert's bangs.

Art Deco A style of architecture and design originating at the Paris Exposition des Arts Décoratifs (1925) and continuing through the 1930s. Art Deco concentrates on simplified geometric forms.

Bias Cut A method of cutting fabric across the grain, devised in the late twenties by Madame Madeleine Vionnet. Panels of fabric cut on the bias and stitched together made dresses cling in certain areas, like the bust and hips, but also created long sweeping skirts that flared out from the thighs.

Chanel, Gabrielle ("Coco") (1883–1971)
French designer, who began working under her own name in 1914. In 1930 Chanel went to Hollywood to design for several films made by United Artists. In 1931 she showed a range of evening dresses designed to promote cotton as a fashion fabric. Much of her attention in the mid-thirties was focused on manufacturing. In 1939 she closed her salon in Paris but reopened it in 1954, at the age of 71.

Cocteau, Jean (1889–1963) French artist, stage designer, illustrator, poet, and playwright. Closely associated with the fashion world through his links with the theater and his friendship with Elsa Schiaparelli, with whom he collaborated on designs for accessories. As an illustrator, Cocteau also designed covers for a number of fashion magazines, notably *Harper's Bazaar*.

Dalí, Salvador (1907–1987) Spanish-born painter and Surrealist, famous for his dreamlike landscapes and images such as melting watches. In addition to designing fabrics for Schiaparelli, Dalí also contributed to jewelry and fashion design.

Dirndl Originally a peasant garment, thought to have originated in the Austrian Tyrol. Dirndls have full skirts, loosely gathered onto a waistband to fall in soft pleats. In the thirties, the popularity of walking and hiking made dirndl skirts fashionable wear.

Ferragamo, Salvatore (1898–1960) Italian shoe designer. At the age of 16, Ferragamo joined his brothers in California where he made shoes by hand for the American film company, Universal Studios, Warner Bros, and MGM, as well as for private clients. Returning to Italy in 1927, in 1936 he set up a workshop in Florence to be the first large-scale producer of handmade shoes. In 1938, Ferragamo was credited as having originated the wedge heel and platform sole.

Halter-neck Created by the high panel of the front of a dress or blouse being tied around the neck, leaving the back and shoulders exposed. The halter neck is credited to Madame Madeleine Vionnet and was popular for evening wear and beach clothes in the 1930s.

Head, Edith (1899–1981) American costume designer and head designer at Hollywood's Paramount studios from 1938 to 1967. With over a thousand film credits, Head designed for Marlene Dietrich, Mae West, and Dorothy Lamour, for whom she designed a sarong in 1936 (for the film *Jungle Princess*) that was widely copied as beachwear.

Lacoste, René (1905–1996) French tennis star, nicknamed "le Crocodile", launched a white, short-sleeved tennis shirt that had a small collar, buttons at the neck, and a small crocodile emblem on the chest (often called an alligator shirt).

Lastex Trade name of the American Rubber Company's elastic yarn made of rubber combined with silk, cotton, or rayon and used for lingerie and swimwear.

Mainbocher (1891–1976) American-born designer, who was a fashion editor in his early career. He gained international publicity when he created a wedding gown for Mrs. Wallis Simpson for her marriage to the Duke of Windsor and created a vogue for Wallis Blue.

Plus-fours Knickers made of tweed or worsted and originally favored by golfers, plus-fours were popular menswear in the thirties, particularly for those favoring automobile driving as a pastime.

Rayon An artificial silk made of cellulose fibers. Rayon draped well and could also be dyed. In 1912 the first rayon stockings were made. In 1916, knitted rayon became popular, and,since it looked and felt like silk, it was a popular substitute in the production of less expensive lingerie.

Schiaparelli, Elsa (1890–1973) Italian-born designer. After spending her early married life in Boston and New York, in 1920 Schiaparelli moved to Paris. In 1929 she opened her own salon specializing in evening wear, tailored clothes, and sportswear. She often collaborated with leading artists like Salvador Dalí and Jean Cocteau, and many of her designs were inspired by Surrealism. She also launched a range of fragrances and cosmetics.

Stiebel, Victor (1907–1976) South African-born designer. While studying at Cambridge in England, Stiebel designed costumes and scenery for the Footlights Revue in London. In 1929 he became an apprentice at the London couture house of Reville and Rossiter, which specialized in formal gowns for clients of the royalty and aristocracy. In 1932 Stiebel opened his own house and, in addition to producing bias-cut evening gowns, he also produced romantic dresses for stage and screen actresses. Experiments in synthetic fabrics led to the creation in 1936 of a taffeta and cellophane gown for Hollywood film star Vivien Leigh.

Surrealism An art movement started in the 1920s and founded by André Breton. The leading artists of the movement were Salvador Dali, René Magritte, Man Ray, Max Ernst, Francis Picabia, and Jean Cocteau. Writers involved included Paul Eluard and Louis Aragon.

Vionnet, Madeleine (Madame) (1876-1975) French-born designer. One of the most innovative designers of her day, Vionnet is credited with the introduction of the bias-cutting technique, the popularization of the halter neck and cowl neck. Vionnet conceived her designs on miniature models, draping fabrics into sinuous folds.

Further Reading

A great deal has been written and published about the 1930s—this reading list is only a very small selection. Magazines and movies of the period are another excellent source of information.

Adult General Reference Sources

Blum, Stella. *Everyday Fashions of the Thirties* (Dover, 1986)

Calasibetta, Charlotte. *Essential Terms of Fashion: A Collection of Definitions* (Fairchild, 1985)

Calasibetta, Charlotte. *Fairchild's Dictionary of Fashion* (Fairchild, 2nd ed, 1988)

Cumming, Valerie. *Understanding Fashion History* (Chrysalis, 2004)

Ewing, Elizabeth. *History of Twentieth Century Fashion*, revised by Alice Mackrell (Batsford, 4th ed, 2001)

Gold, Annalee. *90 Years of Fashion* (Fairchild, 1990)

Laver, James. *Costume and Fashion* (Thames & Hudson, 1995)

Lussier, Suzanne. *Art Deco Fashion* (Bulfinch, 2003)

Martin, Richard. *American Ingenuity: Sportswear* 1930s-1970s (Yale, 1998)

O'Hara, Georgina. *The Encyclopedia of Fashion* (Harry N. Abrams, 1986)

Peacock, John. *Twentieth Century Fashion: The Complete Sourcebook* (Thames & Hudson, 1993)

Peacock, John. *Fashion Sourcebook: The Thirties* (Thames & Hudson, 1997)

Peacock, John. *Men's Fashion: The Complete Sourcebook* (Emerald, 1997)

Peacock, John. *Fashion Accessories: The Complete 20th-century Sourcebook* (Thames & Hudson, 2000)

Stegemeyer, Anne. *Who's Who in Fashion*, (Fairchild, 4th ed, 2003)

Trahey, Jane (ed.) *100 Years of the American Female from Harper's Bazaar* (Random House, 1967)

Watson, Linda. *Twentieth-century Fashion* (Firefly, 2004)

Young Adult Sources

Blackman, Cally. *Twentieth-century Fashion: The 20s and 30s* (Heinemann Library, 1999)

Ruby, Jennifer. *The Nineteen Twenties & Nineteen Thirties, Costume in Context series* (David & Charles, 1989)

Wilcox, R. Turner. *Five Centuries of American Costume* (Scribner's, 1963)

Acknowledgments

The Publishers would like to thank the following for permission to reproduce illustrations: Advertising Archive 40; Aquascutum 56; Art Archive 13, 20l, 24r, 34l, 35, 36, 38b, 38t, 39tl; Art Archive/DACS 25, 48tl; B.T. Batsford 28t, 31t, 31b, 37r, 39r 43t, 44r, 45r, 46, 48r, 49, 50l, 52t, 55t, 57bl, 57tl; Getty Images 21t, 21b, 22, 26, 54t; Greyhound Bus Co. 38c; Kobal Collection 12r, 14t, 24l, 32t, 33b, 33t, 41, 43b, 53b; Library of Congress 27; Mary Evans Picture Library 7, 9, 10, 11, 12l, 15, 16tl, 18, 19b, 23, 29tl, 29tr, 37l, 42l, 42r, 44l, 45bl, 45tl, 47r, 48bl, 50br, 51, 52b, 54b, 55b, 57tr, 58br, 58t, 59; National Film Archive 30; Popperfoto 34r; Retrograph 16r; Topfoto 6, 8, 14b, 16bl, 17r, 19t, 20r, 29b, 32b, 47l, 53t; Vintage Magazine Co. 17l, 28b, 39bl, 50tr, 58bl

Key: b=bottom, t=top, l=left, r=right

Index

Numbers in *italics* refer to illustrations